Crypto Chaos: The Rise and Fall of Binance

Unraveling the Billion-Dollar Empire, Money Laundering Scandals, and the Battle for Crypto Compliance

Daniel Allen

Copyright © 2023 by Daniel Allen

This book is a work of non-fiction and is based on extensive research and interviews conducted by the author. While every effort has been made to ensure the accuracy of the information presented, the author and publisher cannot be held responsible for any errors or omissions, or for any consequences arising from the use of the information contained in this book.

Table of Contents

INTRODUCTION

The modern-day financial environment has been changed by cryptocurrencies, where globalized, decentralized transactional systems are created. The introduction goes further into the basic notions of the crypto world, considers what makes Binance a vital actor in it, and analyzes the benefits as well as the threats that characterize the domain of virtual finance.

Understanding the Crypto Landscape

This phenomenon has since seen the birth of cryptocurrencies that have completely turned the conventional financial systems around. The cryptos are built around a more advanced form of blockchain. These transactions will be secure because no one or even organization will own it. Cryptocurrencies differ from conventional currencies in that they run on a peer-to-peer network, which allows individuals to conduct transactions with each other directly without using banks as brokers. Transactions are irreversible and transparent due to blockchain, which represents an unchangeable distributed registry with public accessibility.

Cryptocurrency was introduced when Bitcoin came on board in 2009 through a non-identified party known as Satoshi Nakamoto. It showed that an independent and unregulated currency was possible. Ethereum was another notable figure in blockchain extension that came up with smart contracts—self-enforcing agreements whose terms are contained within the code itself. Crypto space includes numerous coins and tokens having various functions. The idea behind altcoins is to upgrade the shortcomings of bitcoin. This is exemplified by stable coins pegged to traditional currencies offering greater stability in a turbulent environment. Blockchain applications can be seen in initial digital currencies like ICOS and DeFis.

The importance of Binance to the cryptocurrency industry.

One of the many cryptocurrency exchanges, Binance, became prominent and changed the sector topography. Binance was initiated into operation in 2017 by Changpeng Zhao and it is currently regarded as the largest digital money exchange globally according to trade volumes. Moreover, it goes beyond the issue of the market leader; Binance was instrumental in the promotion of crypto-currencies and making them accessible across the globe.

The platform also had an intuitive interface, numerous crypto assets it supported, as well as innovative offerings like future trading that helped set it apart. Its convenience attracted both newcomers in trading and experienced ones, hence it led to the enormous expansion of its user base. The crypto community found a new celebrity in the form of Changpeng Zhao popularly known as CZ, who championed the mainstreaming of Blockchains.

Binace's native token -Binance Coin (BNB)– further strengthened the impact. The BNB made it possible to reduce trading charges across the platform and functioned as the utility token of the entire Binance system. Binance's early success provided a foundation for services such as Binance Launchpad for token launches and Binance Academy for education.

The promise and perils of digital finance

Digital finance holds great promise for improving accessibility, transparency, and inclusion. As a subset of digital finance, cryptocurrencies symbolize this promise of giving financial services to the globally unbanked and underbanked people. Blockchain technology is a decentralized system that will bring more security and more transparency to financial transactions.

Nonetheless, this undertaking holds certain risks. Illegal acts, such as money laundering, fraudulent transactions, and ransomware are also perpetrated through cryptocurrencies which lack centralization and anonymity. Poor regulation in the first years of the crypto bubble allowed criminal elements to abuse the system. In this changing terrain, crypto's on-ramp, or the cryptocurrency exchange, also had a dual role of facilitator and battlefield.

The success of Binance represents everything about the crypto industry's rapid growth, as well as its pitfalls. The world of cryptocurrency was promised accessibility by its user-friendly interface, but money laundering procedures breaches plus the accusations made it problematic. However, at the face of it, digital finance seems a contradiction in that while on one hand, it aims to liberate persons on the other, it tends to challenge established regulatory systems.

Throughout these chapters, we unfold the intricate tale of how Binance came into existence and fell into disgrace. The journey will explore the complex nature of crypto-culture, the implications of regulation, and the changing space of digital money.

Chapter 1: Binance Genesis

In the dynamic realm of cryptocurrency, the emergence of Binance marked a pivotal moment that would reshape the landscape. This chapter embarks on a journey through the genesis of Binance, exploring the inception of the exchange, the visionary leader behind its creation—Changpeng Zhao (CZ)—and the remarkable trajectory that propelled it to crypto dominance.

The Birth of Binance and Changpeng Zhao

The year 2017 witnessed the birth of Binance, a cryptocurrency exchange founded by the enigmatic Changpeng Zhao. CZ, as he is widely known in the crypto community, brought a unique blend of expertise and vision to the table. His background included stints at notable financial institutions, including Bloomberg Tradebook and OKCoin, where he gained valuable insights into the intricacies of the financial world. The genesis of Binance was rooted in CZ's deep understanding of the challenges faced by existing cryptocurrency exchanges. He envisioned a platform that would not only address these challenges but also set new standards for user experience and efficiency. The name "Binance," a fusion of "binary" and "finance," encapsulated the exchange's commitment to the digital nature of cryptocurrencies and the financial services it aimed to provide.

The early days of Binance were characterized by a relentless focus on innovation and a commitment to creating a platform that would stand out in a rapidly growing and competitive market. The exchange's mission was clear: to offer users a seamless and user-friendly experience in the world of digital assets.

Early Growth and the Ascent to Crypto Dominance

Binance's ascent to crypto dominance was nothing short of meteoric. In its initial phase, the exchange introduced several groundbreaking features that set it apart from its peers. Perhaps one of the most noteworthy elements was the introduction of Binance Coin (BNB), the platform's native cryptocurrency.

BNB served a dual purpose within the Binance ecosystem. Firstly, it provided users with a means to reduce trading fees—a practical incentive that resonated with the trading community. Secondly, BNB became a vital component for participating in various activities within the Binance platform, fostering an engaged and active user base. The strategic introduction of BNB was indicative of Binance's commitment to creating a holistic ecosystem that went beyond basic trading functionalities. This move not only contributed to Binance's popularity but also showcased the exchange's forward-thinking approach to incorporating native tokens.

Binance's commitment to enhancing user experience was evident in its robust matching engine, capable of handling a high volume of transactions with minimal latency. This technological prowess, combined with a vast array of supported cryptocurrencies, attracted traders globally, positioning Binance as a go-to platform for crypto enthusiasts. The exchange's strategy of proactively listing promising tokens before they gained widespread recognition further solidified its position in the industry.

Binance became a trendsetter, shaping the direction of the cryptocurrency market by identifying and supporting projects with potential.

Binance's Unique Approach to Global Expansion

What set Binance apart was not only its commitment to innovation but also its unique approach to global expansion. While many exchanges initially focused on specific regions, Binance adopted a global mindset from its inception. The platform was designed to be accessible to users worldwide, with support for multiple languages and a user interface that catered to a diverse international audience.

Binance's global expansion strategy extended beyond linguistic considerations. Recognizing the importance of adhering to regional regulations, the exchange took a proactive approach to compliance. This commitment to regulatory compliance, combined with a robust security framework, not only instilled confidence among users but also positioned Binance as a responsible player in the industry.

To bridge the gap between traditional and digital finance, Binance introduced fiat-to-crypto gateways. This strategic move allowed users to seamlessly convert traditional currencies into cryptocurrencies, facilitating a smoother entry into the world of digital assets. By doing so, Binance became a bridge between the fiat and crypto realms, making cryptocurrencies more accessible to individuals around the globe.

As Binance expanded globally, it formed strategic partnerships and collaborations with local entities. This collaborative approach not only facilitated smoother operations in different regions but also demonstrated Binance's commitment to integrating with the broader financial ecosystem.

The genesis of Binance, characterized by innovation, strategic vision, and a commitment to global accessibility, laid the foundation for its unprecedented growth. The subsequent chapters will delve deeper into the challenges, controversies, and ultimately, the transformative impact that Binance had on the cryptocurrency industry.

Chapter 2: Crypto Empire Unveiled

As Binance entered the crypto arena, it unveiled a disruptive force that would reshape the industry's landscape. This chapter delves into the intricacies of Binance's business model and operations, explores the rapid ascent that crowned it as the world's largest cryptocurrency exchange and provides insight into the visionary leadership style of its founder, Changpeng Zhao.

Binance's Business Model and Operations

At the core of Binance's meteoric rise lies a robust and innovative business model. Unlike traditional financial institutions, Binance operates as a cryptocurrency-to-cryptocurrency exchange. Users can trade various digital assets directly, offering a vast selection of trading pairs that go beyond the limitations of fiat currency-based exchanges. The heart of Binance's operations is its native token, Binance Coin (BNB). Beyond its utility in reducing trading fees for users, BNB plays a crucial role within the Binance ecosystem. It serves as fuel for the Binance Smart Chain (BSC), Binance's blockchain network that facilitates the creation of decentralized applications (DApps) and smart contracts. BNB's dual functionality not only enhances the user experience but also contributes to the overall sustainability of the Binance platform.

Binance's commitment to user security is evident in its implementation of industry-leading measures. The platform employs a multi-tier and multi-cluster system architecture to ensure the stability and security of its operations. Furthermore, Binance incorporates advanced encryption techniques to safeguard user data, providing a secure environment for traders to engage in the dynamic world of cryptocurrencies.

One of the unique features that set Binance apart is its emphasis on fostering innovation within the crypto space. Binance Launchpad, an exclusive token launch platform, provides a launchpad for innovative blockchain projects. This not only allows promising projects to gain exposure but also aligns with Binance's vision of supporting and driving advancements within the crypto industry.

The Rapid Rise to Becoming the World's Largest Crypto Exchange

Binance's journey to becoming the world's largest cryptocurrency exchange was marked by unprecedented growth and an unwavering commitment to excellence. Within a remarkably short period, Binance disrupted the established order of the crypto exchange landscape, surpassing competitors and setting new industry standards.

One of the key contributors to Binance's rapid rise was its user-centric approach. The exchange focused on providing an intuitive and seamless user experience, catering to both novice and experienced traders. The user-friendly interface, combined with a wide array of supported cryptocurrencies, attracted a diverse user base from around the globe. The introduction of innovative features further fueled Binance's ascent. Binance Futures, for instance, allowed users to engage in futures trading with leverage, adding a layer of sophistication to the platform. The availability of a variety of trading pairs and advanced trading tools empowered users to execute their trading strategies with precision.

Binance's strategic approach to listing new tokens played a pivotal role in its growth. By being proactive in identifying and supporting promising projects, Binance became a launchpad for innovative blockchain initiatives. This strategy not only attracted new projects seeking exposure but also positioned Binance as a thought leader in the crypto space.

The strategic use of BNB, the platform's native token, contributed significantly to Binance's growth. BNB not only incentivized users through reduced trading fees but also facilitated the expansion of the Binance ecosystem. The token's adoption as a means of transaction within the platform added a layer of utility that further solidified Binance's position in the crypto world.

Zhao's Vision and Leadership Style

At the helm of Binance stands Changpeng Zhao, the visionary leader whose strategic vision and leadership style played a pivotal role in the platform's success. Known as CZ in the crypto community, Zhao's journey is intertwined with the exponential growth of Binance. Zhao's vision for Binance extended beyond creating a conventional cryptocurrency exchange. He envisioned a comprehensive ecosystem that not only facilitated trading but also contributed to the broader development of blockchain technology. This visionary outlook led to the creation of the Binance Smart Chain (BSC), a blockchain network that complements Binance's trading platform and fosters the growth of decentralized applications.

The leadership style of Zhao is characterized by adaptability and responsiveness to market dynamics. In the fast-paced world of cryptocurrencies, where change is constant, Zhao's ability to navigate uncertainties and make swift decisions has been a driving force behind Binance's agility and resilience.

Zhao's approachability and engagement with the crypto community have been instrumental in fostering trust and transparency. His active presence on social media platforms, including Twitter, where he interacts directly with users, reflects a commitment to open communication. This direct engagement has not only endeared Zhao to the crypto community but has also provided a human touch to the leadership of Binance.

In addition to his commitment to innovation and user satisfaction, Zhao's leadership is marked by a global mindset. Binance's rapid expansion to serve users worldwide reflects Zhao's vision of creating a platform that transcends geographical boundaries. His leadership has played a crucial role in establishing Binance as a global leader in the cryptocurrency industry.

In conclusion, Chapter 2 unveils the inner workings of Binance's crypto empire. From its innovative business model and operational intricacies to the visionary leadership of Changpeng Zhao, this chapter provides a comprehensive understanding of the factors that propelled Binance to its position as the world's largest cryptocurrency exchange. The subsequent chapters will delve into the challenges and controversies that accompanied Binance's journey, ultimately leading to a watershed moment in the cryptocurrency industry.

Chapter 3: The Allegations Surface

In the turbulent narrative of Binance, Chapter 3 unfolds a critical juncture as allegations of money laundering cast a shadow over the once-revered cryptocurrency exchange. This chapter delves into the emergence of money laundering allegations, the uncovering of Binance's anti-money laundering failures, and the initiation of investigations that would become a tipping point for the platform.

Emergence of Money Laundering Allegations

The cryptocurrency industry, often praised for its decentralization and privacy features, found itself under scrutiny as money laundering allegations surfaced against Binance. The exchange, once celebrated for its rapid ascent and innovative approach, now faced a formidable challenge to its reputation. The allegations centered around the claim that Binance had become a haven for illicit activities, ranging from money laundering to terrorist financing. Authorities asserted that bad actors were freely engaging in transactions on the platform, facilitating a range of criminal activities, including child sex abuse, narcotics trade, and funding for notorious groups like ISIS, Al Qaeda, and Hamas's Al-Qassam Brigades.

The emergence of these allegations sent shockwaves through the cryptocurrency community and beyond. Binance touted as a trailblazer in the industry, now found itself at the center of one of the most significant controversies in the crypto space.

Uncovering Binance's Anti-Money Laundering Failures

As the allegations gained traction, a spotlight was cast on Binance's anti-money laundering (AML) practices or the lack thereof. Authorities alleged that the exchange had not only failed to implement effective AML measures but had also turned a blind eye to its legal obligations in pursuit of profits.

The accusations suggested that Binance knowingly allowed transactions involving illicit activities, providing a platform for criminals to move their funds with impunity. The absence of robust AML procedures, it was claimed, created an environment conducive to criminal elements, enabling them to exploit the platform for their illicit financial activities. In a particularly damning revelation, court records unveiled a deliberate and calculated effort by Binance to profit from the U.S. market without implementing the necessary controls mandated by U.S. laws. This revelation indicated a systemic failure in compliance, raising questions about the exchange's commitment to regulatory adherence.

Investigations Begin: A Tipping Point for Binance

In the wake of the money laundering allegations, investigations were initiated by various government agencies, marking a significant tipping point for Binance. The U.S. Department of Justice, the Treasury's Financial Crimes Enforcement Network (FinCEN), the Office of Foreign Asset Controls (OFAC), and the Commodity Futures Trading Commission

(CFTC) collectively launched an inquiry into the exchange's operations. The scale of the investigations was unprecedented, reflecting the severity of the allegations against Binance. Authorities sought to ascertain the extent of the exchange's involvement in facilitating illicit transactions and whether its practices violated U.S. laws and regulations.

The allegations came to a head as Binance admitted to engaging in anti-money laundering, unlicensed money transmitting, and sanctions violations. In a coordinated settlement across the federal government, Binance agreed to pay a staggering $4 billion in fines and penalties. This marked the largest-ever corporate resolution that included criminal charges for an executive in the cryptocurrency industry.

Zhao Changpeng, the founder and CEO of Binance, faced personal consequences as well.

Pleading guilty to failing to maintain an effective anti-money laundering program, Zhao agreed to step down from his position at the helm of the exchange. The financial penalties imposed on Zhao, totaling $200 million, underscored the gravity of the allegations and the accountability sought by U.S. authorities.

The investigations not only revealed the extent of Binance's lapses in compliance but also exposed the platform's complicity in facilitating illicit activities. The U.S. authorities aimed to send a clear message to bad actors across the crypto industry that non-compliance with regulations would not be tolerated.

In a post on social media, Zhao confirmed his decision to step down, acknowledging mistakes and expressing a commitment to taking responsibility for the platform's past actions. The leadership vacuum left by Zhao's departure raised questions about the future trajectory of

Binance and the industry-wide impact of the investigations.

As Chapter 3 comes to a close, the once-mighty Binance stands at a crossroads, grappling with the repercussions of money laundering allegations and the weight of historic penalties. The subsequent chapters will unravel the aftermath of the investigations, exploring the industry's response, regulatory implications, and the enduring impact on Binance's legacy in the cryptocurrency world.

Chapter 4: Crimes on the Blockchain

As the legal saga surrounding Binance unfolded, this chapter delves into the grim reality of crimes on the blockchain. Prosecutors unveil a tapestry of unlawful activities, exposing the dark side of crypto—from child abuse to terrorism financing. This chapter peels back the layers to examine Binance's role in facilitating illicit transactions, shedding light on a troubling intersection between the cryptocurrency industry and criminal endeavors.

Prosecutors Unveil Binance's Unlawful Activities

The legal scrutiny surrounding Binance brought to light a myriad of unlawful activities facilitated by the cryptocurrency exchange. Prosecutors, armed with evidence gathered during extensive investigations, painted a damning picture of the exchange's involvement in a spectrum of crimes.

Court records unsealed during legal proceedings detailed Binance's processing of transactions by customers engaged in illicit mixing services. These services, prosecutors alleged, were conduits for laundering proceeds from darknet market transactions, hacks, ransomware, and scams. The exchange's lax anti-money laundering (AML) procedures were cited as a contributing factor to the success of these illicit activities. Prosecutors asserted that

Binance's deliberate failure to register as a money service business and its willful violation of the Bank Secrecy Act were central to its ability to operate as a hub for criminal transactions. The accusations painted a portrait of a platform that prioritized growth, market share, and profits over compliance with U.S. laws—a choice that would have far-reaching consequences.

The unfolding legal proceedings exposed a deliberate and calculated effort by Binance to profit from the U.S. market without implementing the controls mandated by U.S. laws. A compliance employee's message, revealed during the investigations, humorously encapsulated the allegations: "Is washing drug money too hard these days? Come to Binance, we got cake for you." This stark revelation further underscored the gravity of the allegations against the exchange.

The Dark Side of Crypto: From Child Abuse to Terrorism Financing

The allegations against Binance transcended conventional financial crimes, delving into the darkest corners of the crypto landscape. Prosecutors outlined the platform's complicity in facilitating a range of heinous activities, including child sex abuse, narcotics trade, and financing for notorious terrorist organizations such as ISIS, Al Qaeda, and Hamas's Al-Qassam Brigades.

The unearthing of Binance's role in these activities sent shockwaves through the crypto community and beyond. The anonymity and pseudonymity afforded by blockchain technology, once touted as a strength of cryptocurrencies, had become a double-edged sword. While providing privacy for legitimate users, it also offered a veil for criminals to operate beyond the reach of traditional law enforcement. The exploitation of cryptocurrencies for nefarious purposes had been a growing concern, and the Binance case brought this issue to the forefront. The intersection of crypto and criminal activities, ranging from the most abhorrent forms of exploitation to acts of terrorism, underscored the urgent need for robust regulatory frameworks and enhanced industry diligence.

Binance's Role in Facilitating Illicit Transactions

Binance's alleged role in facilitating illicit transactions extended beyond inadvertent oversight. Prosecutors contended that the exchange knowingly turned a blind eye to its legal obligations, creating an environment where criminals could freely transact. The absence of a robust AML program and the failure to implement necessary controls enabled bad actors to exploit the platform for their criminal enterprises. The charges outlined more than 100,000 transactions involving illicit activity, ranging from darknet market transactions to ransomware actions. Additionally, prosecutors highlighted more than 1.5 million virtual currency trades that violated U.S. sanctions, including those imposed on nations like Iran, Syria, and Cuba.

The allegations against Binance suggested a willful disregard for the consequences of its actions, with the exchange accused of prioritizing profit over compliance with U.S. laws. The immense scale of illicit transactions raised questions about the platform's commitment to the safety and security of the broader financial system.

As the curtain fell on the revelations of crimes on the blockchain, the cryptocurrency industry faced a reckoning. Binance, once a symbol of innovation and success, now stood accused of being an unwitting accomplice to a spectrum of criminal activities. The subsequent chapters will navigate the aftermath of these revelations, exploring the implications for the broader crypto industry, the response of regulatory bodies, and the enduring impact on the perception of cryptocurrencies in the global financial landscape.

Chapter 5: Legal Battles and Regulatory Scrutiny

As the Binance saga unfolded, Chapter 5 chronicles the legal battles and regulatory scrutiny that defined a pivotal moment in the history of the cryptocurrency industry. The chapter unravels the intense confrontation between Binance and regulatory authorities, the coordinated investigation by the U.S. government, and the far-reaching impact on other cryptocurrency exchanges.

Binance vs. Regulatory Authorities

The legal battles between Binance and regulatory authorities marked a turning point in the relationship between the cryptocurrency industry and government oversight. Binance once considered a trailblazer and a symbol of crypto innovation, found itself at odds with regulatory frameworks designed to ensure transparency, compliance, and the safeguarding of financial systems.

The U.S. Securities and Exchange Commission (SEC) had already initiated civil cases against Binance, accusing the exchange of running an illegal exchange for unregistered securities in the United States. The legal tussle unfolded on multiple fronts, with allegations of an extensive web of deception, conflicts of interest, lack of disclosure, and calculated evasion of the law.

Binance, however, had long maintained that it wasn't subject to U.S. laws due to the absence of a physical headquarters in America. The platform's decentralized nature became a focal point in the legal arguments, challenging conventional notions of jurisdiction in the digital age. The SEC further alleged that Zhao Changpeng and Binance commingled customer assets, diverting some to an entity controlled by Zhao. This revelation added another layer to the legal quagmire, as regulators sought to untangle the complex web of financial transactions associated with the exchange.

The legal battles underscored broader questions about the regulatory framework for cryptocurrencies. While proponents argued for a balance between innovation and regulation, critics contended that the crypto industry needed more robust oversight to prevent abuses and protect investors.

The U.S. Government's Coordinated Investigation

Amidst the legal battles, the U.S. government orchestrated a coordinated investigation into Binance that involved multiple agencies. The Department of Justice, the Treasury's Financial Crimes Enforcement Network (FinCEN), the Office of Foreign Asset Controls (OFAC), and the Commodity Futures Trading Commission (CFTC) collaborated to scrutinize various aspects of the exchange's operations.

This coordinated effort represented one of the most significant regulatory actions in the history of the cryptocurrency industry. The government's intent was clear: to hold Binance accountable for alleged violations ranging from anti-money laundering failures to sanctions violations. The investigation delved into Binance's business model, operational practices, and compliance measures. The revelations from this inquiry formed the basis for the subsequent legal actions and settlements that would reshape the landscape for cryptocurrency exchanges.

The U.S. government's involvement sent a strong signal to the broader crypto industry. It signaled a commitment to enforcing existing laws and regulations, regardless of the decentralized and borderless nature of cryptocurrencies. The industry, which had operated in a relatively unregulated environment, now faced the prospect of increased scrutiny and accountability.

Impact on Other Cryptocurrency Exchanges

The ripple effects of the Binance investigation reverberated across the cryptocurrency landscape, impacting other exchanges and prompting a reevaluation of compliance measures industry-wide. The unprecedented scale of the allegations and the subsequent penalties imposed on Binance served as a cautionary tale for crypto platforms worldwide.

Cryptocurrency exchanges faced increased pressure to enhance their AML procedures, implement effective compliance measures, and ensure adherence to regulatory requirements. The Binance case became a focal point for regulators globally, influencing discussions about the need for standardized regulations to govern the burgeoning crypto industry.

Some exchanges took proactive steps, voluntarily improving their compliance frameworks to avoid potential legal pitfalls. The industry once celebrated for its autonomy, now grappled with the reality that regulatory compliance was essential for long-term sustainability and legitimacy.

As the chapter concludes, the legal battles and regulatory scrutiny surrounding Binance reshaped the narrative for the cryptocurrency industry. The clash between innovation and regulation reached a critical juncture, forcing stakeholders to confront the challenges of balancing technological advancement with the need for robust oversight. The subsequent chapters will explore the aftermath of these legal battles, examining the evolving regulatory landscape and its implications for the future of cryptocurrencies.

Chapter 6: The Guilty Plea

In this we unfurl the dramatic developments leading to Binance's guilty plea—a seismic moment that reshaped the cryptocurrency landscape. This chapter delves into Binance's admission of wrongdoing, the consequential decision by Changpeng Zhao to step down, and the intricate details of the coordinated settlement and fines that would leave an indelible mark on the crypto industry.

Binance's Admission of Wrongdoing

In a watershed moment for the cryptocurrency industry, Binance made a stunning admission of wrongdoing. The exchange once hailed as a pioneer in the crypto space, acknowledged engaging in anti-money laundering (AML) violations, unlicensed money transmitting, and sanctions violations. This unprecedented confession reverberated across the financial world, signaling a paradigm shift in the way cryptocurrency platforms were held accountable for their actions. Binance's admission laid bare the extent of its lapses in compliance and regulatory adherence. The acknowledgment of AML failures was particularly significant, as it implicated the exchange in facilitating illicit transactions, ranging from child sex abuse to terrorism financing. The admission punctured the veil of invincibility that had shrouded Binance, forcing a reckoning with the consequences of its actions.

The industry, once characterized by a degree of defiance against traditional regulatory norms, now witnessed a major player humbled by the weight of its transgressions. Binance's admission underscored the growing importance of regulatory compliance in the cryptocurrency sector and set a precedent for other platforms to reassess their practices.

Changpeng Zhao Steps Down: The End of an Era

In tandem with Binance's admission, Changpeng Zhao, the charismatic founder and CEO, announced his decision to step down. Zhao, often regarded as one of the most powerful figures in the crypto world, acknowledged the need for accountability and leadership change in the wake of the guilty plea. This moment marked the end of an era for Binance. Zhao, who had steered the exchange through unprecedented growth and challenges, faced the consequences of the platform's transgressions under his leadership. His decision to step down sent shockwaves through the cryptocurrency community, as industry observers grappled with the fall of a once-untouchable icon.

Zhao's departure left a leadership vacuum at Binance, prompting questions about the future trajectory of the exchange and its ability to recover from the reputational and financial blows. The charismatic CEO, known for his bold vision and unyielding commitment to the principles of decentralization, bowed out under the weight of regulatory scrutiny and the looming specter of legal repercussions.

Details of the Coordinated Settlement and Fines

The guilty plea ushered in a coordinated settlement that reverberated with historic significance. Binance agreed to pay more than $4 billion in fines and other penalties—an astronomical sum that underscored the severity of the allegations and the scale of regulatory repercussions. This marked the largest-ever corporate resolution that included criminal charges for an executive in the cryptocurrency industry.

Changpeng Zhao, facing personal accountability, agreed to a staggering $200 million in fines. The fines were not merely symbolic; they reflected the tangible consequences of the platform's actions and sent a resounding message to other industry players about the high stakes of regulatory non-compliance.

The details of the settlement outlined a comprehensive response from various U.S. government agencies, including the Department of Justice, the Treasury's Financial Crimes Enforcement Network (FinCEN), the Office of Foreign Asset Controls (OFAC), and the Commodity Futures Trading Commission

(CFTC). The coordinated effort showcased the determination of regulatory bodies to hold Binance accountable for a range of violations, from anti-money laundering to sanctions breaches.

As part of the settlement, Binance agreed to disgorge $1.35 billion of ill-gotten gains and pay a $1.35 billion civil monetary penalty to the CFTC. The financial implications of the settlement sent shockwaves through the cryptocurrency industry, prompting a reassessment of risk management and compliance measures across exchanges.

In a post on social media, Changpeng Zhao reflected on the difficulty of letting go emotionally but emphasized the necessity of the decision for the community, Binance, and himself. The charismatic leader, who had navigated Binance through rapid global expansion, acknowledged mistakes and took responsibility for the platform's past actions.

As Chapter 6 concludes, Binance stands at a crossroads, grappling with the fallout of a guilty plea, leadership change, and unprecedented financial penalties. The subsequent chapters will explore the aftermath of this pivotal moment, examining the industry's response, regulatory adaptations, and the enduring impact on Binance's legacy in the cryptocurrency world.

Chapter 7: The Fallout

In the aftermath of Binance's seismic scandal and guilty plea, Chapter 7 unfolds to dissect the profound consequences that rippled through the cryptocurrency industry. This chapter scrutinizes the market's reaction to Binance's transgressions, the overarching repercussions for the broader crypto landscape, and the invaluable lessons learned as the industry grapples with the imperative to fortify compliance measures.

Market Reaction to Binance's Scandal

As news of Binance's guilty plea reverberated through financial markets, the cryptocurrency industry experienced a seismic shift in dynamics. The market, once fueled by unbridled enthusiasm for decentralized finance and borderless transactions, now grappled with the sobering reality that even the giants of the sector were not immune to regulatory scrutiny.

In the immediate aftermath, Binance's native cryptocurrency, BNB, faced a precipitous decline in value. Investors, alarmed by the unprecedented fines and the departure of Changpeng Zhao, exhibited a loss of confidence in the once-dominant exchange. The shockwaves extended beyond BNB, impacting the broader cryptocurrency market as uncertainty and fear permeated investor sentiment.

Volatility, a hallmark of the crypto space, reached new heights as traders sought to navigate the uncertainties introduced by Binance's fall from grace. The scandal prompted a reevaluation of risk in the crypto market, with investors and institutions alike reassessing their exposure to platforms that might attract regulatory scrutiny.

The market's reaction to Binance's scandal underscored the interconnectedness of the crypto ecosystem. The downfall of a major exchange sent reverberations through various altcoins and projects associated with Binance, emphasizing the need for diversification and risk management in the crypto investment landscape.

Repercussions for the Cryptocurrency Industry

Beyond the immediate market reactions, the repercussions of Binance's scandal echoed across the broader cryptocurrency industry. Regulatory authorities globally intensified their scrutiny of crypto exchanges, signaling a new era of heightened oversight and accountability. The Binance case served as a precedent, illustrating the potential consequences for platforms that failed to prioritize regulatory compliance.

Several countries, prompted by Binance's legal troubles, revisited their approach to cryptocurrency regulation. Some jurisdictions sought to tighten regulatory frameworks, imposing stricter compliance requirements on exchanges to prevent a recurrence of the alleged transgressions witnessed in the Binance case. The industry found itself at a crossroads, navigating the delicate balance between innovation and the imperative for regulatory adherence. Investors and institutional players, once lured by the promise of unregulated financial freedom in the crypto space, now grappling with the evolving landscape. Due diligence became a focal point for market participants, with increased emphasis on selecting platforms that demonstrated robust compliance measures and a commitment to regulatory cooperation.

The fallout from Binance's scandal also prompted a reevaluation of business models within the crypto industry. Exchanges and projects that had thrived on the peripheries of regulatory oversight now faced a more discerning audience. The onus shifted to the industry's stakeholders to demonstrate a commitment to transparency, security, and adherence to legal and regulatory standards.

Lessons Learned: Strengthening Compliance in the Crypto World

As the dust settled, the cryptocurrency industry confronted a pivotal moment of introspection. Chapter 7 explores the invaluable lessons learned from Binance's scandal and outlines the imperative to strengthen compliance in the crypto world. One of the key takeaways was the recognition that regulatory compliance did not impede innovation but rather a prerequisite for sustainable growth. The crypto industry, propelled by the ethos of decentralization and autonomy, now acknowledged the necessity of collaborating with regulators to foster an environment of trust and legitimacy.

Cryptocurrency exchanges, once celebrated for their agility and independence, found themselves compelled to invest in robust compliance frameworks. The Binance case illustrated that the lack of effective anti-money laundering measures and the willful disregard for regulatory obligations could not only tarnish the reputation of individual platforms but also cast a shadow on the industry as a whole. In response to the lessons learned, industry leaders initiated a paradigm shift toward proactive regulatory engagement. Collaborative efforts between cryptocurrency stakeholders and regulatory bodies gained momentum, signaling a maturation of the industry. The establishment of industry standards for compliance and the development of self-regulatory initiatives emerged as crucial steps toward fostering a more responsible and sustainable crypto ecosystem.

Market participants, armed with the lessons from Binance's downfall, became more discerning in their selection of cryptocurrency projects and exchanges. Due diligence extended beyond the promise of technological innovation to encompass a rigorous assessment of compliance measures, corporate governance, and transparency.

Educational initiatives flourished within the industry, with a renewed focus on raising awareness about the importance of regulatory compliance. Conferences, webinars, and forums became platforms for discussing best practices, navigating legal landscapes, and fostering a culture of responsible innovation.

As Chapter 7 concludes, the cryptocurrency industry emerges from the fallout of Binance's scandal with a heightened awareness of the imperative for compliance. The subsequent chapters will explore the ongoing transformations in the industry, the evolving regulatory landscape, and the enduring impact of this pivotal moment on the trajectory of cryptocurrencies in the global financial ecosystem.

Chapter 8: The Future of Cryptocurrency

As the cryptocurrency industry navigates the aftermath of Binance's scandal, Chapter 8 ventures into the horizon, exploring the future trajectory of digital finance. This chapter probes the arduous task of rebuilding trust after the seismic shockwaves, analyzes the ripple effects of regulatory changes, and envisions the evolving landscape of digital finance in a post-Binance era.

Rebuilding Trust in the Wake of Binance's Scandal

Central to the future of cryptocurrency is the formidable challenge of rebuilding trust, shattered in the wake of Binance's scandal. The once-revered exchange, now synonymous with regulatory transgressions, left a scar on the industry's collective psyche. Chapter 8 delves into the multifaceted approach required to mend this breach of trust. Platforms within the crypto space, cognizant of the skepticism now surrounding the industry, embarked on transparency initiatives. Detailed disclosures of compliance measures, security protocols, and regulatory adherence became paramount. Exchanges sought to demystify their operations, assuring users and investors that lessons from Binance's downfall had catalyzed a paradigm shift toward accountability.

Educational campaigns played a pivotal role in rebuilding trust. Cryptocurrency organizations, industry associations, and thought leaders collaborated to disseminate accurate information about the industry's commitment to compliance, innovation, and responsible growth. These initiatives aimed not only to rectify misconceptions but also to foster a more informed and discerning community.

In the crucible of Binance's scandal, industry stakeholders recognized the need for self-regulation. Cryptocurrency exchanges, projects, and associations united to establish industry standards, codes of conduct, and mechanisms for peer review. The goal was to cultivate a culture of accountability within the industry, demonstrating to users, investors, and regulators that the crypto community was proactive in addressing challenges and fortifying the foundations of trust.

The user experience also transformed. Platforms prioritized enhanced security measures, user-friendly interfaces, and clear communication channels. User empowerment became a cornerstone of the rebuilding process, with exchanges and projects actively seeking user feedback and implementing measures to address concerns promptly. The narrative shifted from unchecked autonomy to responsible decentralization.

Regulatory Changes and Their Implications

This chapter scrutinizes the tectonic shifts in regulatory landscapes catalyzed by Binance's scandal and the subsequent industry-wide introspection. Governments and regulatory bodies, prompted by the revelations, embarked on ambitious efforts to refine and codify their stance toward cryptocurrencies.

The United States, in particular, witnessed a surge in legislative proposals aimed at bringing greater clarity to the regulatory treatment of digital assets. Cryptocurrency exchanges faced heightened scrutiny, and proposals for comprehensive frameworks to govern the sector gained traction. The implications of these regulatory changes extended far beyond U.S. borders, influencing global conversations about the future of crypto regulation.

Other jurisdictions, buoyed by the lessons from Binance's case, engaged in collaborative efforts to create international standards for cryptocurrency regulation. Forums and working groups emerged, fostering dialogue between regulators from different countries. The ambition was to establish a harmonized regulatory framework that could navigate the global nature of cryptocurrency transactions while respecting the sovereignty of individual nations.

Regulatory changes also spurred innovations in compliance technology. Cryptocurrency projects and exchanges invested heavily in advanced anti-money laundering (AML) and know-your-customer (KYC) solutions. Decentralized finance (DeFi) platforms, often considered on the fringes of regulatory oversight, faced the imperative to adapt to evolving compliance standards or risk exclusion from mainstream financial systems.

The Evolving Landscape of Digital Finance

The chapter culminates in a panoramic exploration of the evolving landscape of digital finance. The aftermath of Binance's scandal acted as a catalyst for transformative shifts that reverberated beyond compliance and regulation.

Decentralized finance (DeFi) projects, once seen as disruptors challenging traditional financial institutions, now sought integration with existing regulatory frameworks. The maturation of DeFi involved a delicate dance between innovation and compliance, as projects endeavored to strike a balance between the ethos of decentralization and the regulatory expectations of financial authorities.

Central bank digital currencies (CBDCs) gained prominence as governments contemplated their role in the future of money. The specter of Binance's scandal prompted central banks to expedite their exploration of digital currencies, driven by the recognition that the cryptocurrency industry was evolving rapidly, necessitating a proactive response from traditional financial institutions.

The role of blockchain technology expanded beyond cryptocurrencies, finding applications in supply chain management, healthcare, and governance. As the technology matured, conversations around blockchain's potential to revolutionize industries gained momentum, contributing to a broader acceptance of distributed ledger technology as a transformative force. In the wake of Binance's scandal, investor attitudes toward risk underwent a recalibration. The industry witnessed a shift from speculative fervor to a more discerning approach to investment. Projects and platforms that prioritized transparency, compliance, and long-term sustainability garnered increased attention and support.

As Chapter 8 concludes, the future of cryptocurrency emerges as a dynamic and adaptive landscape. The industry, having weathered the storm of Binance's scandal, faces the future with a heightened awareness of the need for trust, compliance, and responsible innovation. Subsequent chapters will delve into the ongoing transformations, emerging trends, and the enduring impact of this pivotal period on the trajectory of digital finance in the global financial ecosystem.

CONCLUSION

As we draw the final curtain on this exploration of Binance's rise, fall, and profound implications for the cryptocurrency landscape, the concluding chapter invites contemplation on the past, the ongoing evolution of cryptocurrencies, and the intriguing path that lies ahead for the global crypto community.

Reflections on Binance's Rise and Fall

Binance's journey from obscurity to dominance and subsequently to the epicenter of one of the largest scandals in the crypto industry is a narrative laden with lessons and reflections. The ascent of Binance, led by the visionary

Changpeng Zhao, mirrored the exuberance and untamed growth of the broader cryptocurrency space. However, this narrative also underscored the perils of unchecked expansion, the importance of regulatory compliance, and the delicate balance between innovation and responsibility.

The fall of Binance, marked by guilty pleas, staggering fines, and the departure of its charismatic leader, forces us to scrutinize the dynamics that fueled its rise. It prompts an examination of the industry's collective responsibility in fostering a culture of compliance, ethical conduct, and transparency. Binance's story becomes a cautionary tale, a reminder that even the titans of the crypto realm are not immune to the consequences of neglecting foundational principles.

In reflecting on Binance's rise and fall, the industry must grapple with its complicity in enabling unchecked growth. It beckons a collective introspection about the values that should underpin the crypto ecosystem—values that go beyond market dominance and financial success to encompass integrity, accountability, and a commitment to the greater good.

The Ongoing Evolution of Cryptocurrencies

Chapter by chapter, we've traced the intricate narrative of the cryptocurrency industry, a narrative that remains in perpetual motion. As we stand at the crossroads of Binance's tumultuous saga, the ongoing evolution of cryptocurrencies unfolds as a saga of resilience, adaptation, and continuous transformation.

Binance's scandal, though seismic, is but a chapter in the larger story of digital finance.

The industry, known for its capacity to absorb shocks and rebound with newfound vigor, is already undergoing metamorphosis. The decentralized ethos of blockchain technology continues to shape not only the financial sector but various facets of our global landscape.

Decentralized finance (DeFi), once the insurgent challenger to traditional financial institutions, now navigates a delicate dance with regulators. The maturation of DeFi projects underscores a broader trend—innovation within the cryptocurrency space no longer thrives solely on the fringes of regulation but seeks integration and collaboration.

Central bank digital currencies (CBDCs) emerge as pivotal players in the ongoing evolution. Governments, prompted by the lessons of Binance's scandal, accelerate their exploration of digital currencies. The coexistence of traditional fiat currencies and digital counterparts propels the financial ecosystem into uncharted territories, heralding a paradigm shift in the very nature of money.

Blockchain technology, the backbone of cryptocurrencies, extends its influence far beyond digital assets. Its applications in supply chain management, healthcare, and governance underscore the transformative potential that reverberates through industries. The ongoing evolution transcends cryptocurrencies' speculative allure, positioning blockchain as a formidable force for positive change.

In this ongoing narrative, the cryptocurrency industry also grapples with its identity. The community navigates the delicate balance between innovation and regulatory compliance. The once-libertarian ideals of absolute decentralization encounter the pragmatism of collaborative engagement with traditional financial systems. The industry is at an inflection point, shaping its destiny with each code commit, regulatory dialogue, and strategic partnership.

What Lies Ahead for the Global Crypto Community

As we peer into the horizon of the global crypto community, uncertainty mingles with boundless potential. Binance's scandal, rather than marking the demise of the industry, becomes a crucible for transformation. The trajectory that lies ahead hinges on the choices made collectively by industry leaders, regulators, developers, and users.

The global crypto community faces the imperative to chart a course toward a future that embraces innovation without sacrificing integrity. Regulatory frameworks, borne out of the lessons learned from Binance's downfall, crystallize into guiding principles that balance the need for security, consumer protection, and financial inclusion with the industry's inherent dynamism. Education emerges as a linchpin for the future. Cryptocurrency literacy becomes a powerful tool for dismantling misconceptions, fostering responsible participation, and building bridges between traditional financial systems and the decentralized frontier. Industry players invest in initiatives that demystify blockchain, cryptocurrencies, and their potential impact on society.

Collaboration becomes the cornerstone of the global crypto community's resilience. Projects, exchanges, and regulatory bodies engage in open dialogue, working toward standardized practices, interoperability, and frameworks that transcend national borders. The spirit of collaboration extends beyond the industry, forging partnerships with academia, governments, and other sectors to foster a holistic understanding of cryptocurrencies.

In envisioning what lies ahead, the community grapples with the delicate dance between innovation and safeguarding against illicit activities. The evolution of compliance technologies becomes pivotal in ensuring that the crypto landscape remains a hostile terrain for bad actors while preserving the principles of privacy and financial autonomy.

Ultimately, what lies ahead for the global crypto community is a narrative shaped by adaptability, responsibility, and a commitment to the ethos that fueled the inception of cryptocurrencies—the promise of financial inclusion, empowerment, and a decentralized future.

As we close this chapter, the journey of the cryptocurrency industry persists. The enduring impact of Binance's rise and fall becomes a guiding star, illuminating the path toward a future where the global crypto community thrives, evolves, and contributes to reshaping the contours of our financial reality.